Dogspell
The Gospel According to Dog

Dogspell
The Gospel According to Dog

Mary Ellen Ashcroft

Church Publishing
NEW YORK

Church Publishing
19 East 34th Street
New York, NY 10016
www.churchpublishing.org

Cover art: Shutterstock

Cover design: Jennifer Glosser at 2Pug Design

Library of Congress Cataloging-in-Publication Data
Ashcroft, Mary Ellen, 1952–
Dogspell : the Gospel according to dog / Mary Ellen
Ashcroft. — [New ed.].
p. cm.
ISBN 978-1-59627-093-0 (hardcover)
ISBN 978-0-89869-221-1 (pbk.)
1. God (Christianity)—Meditations. 2. Dogs—Religious aspects—
Christianity—
Meditations. I. Title.
BT103.A83 2008
231—dc22

2008012431

Printed in the United States of America

Dedicated to Esme Beverly:
That she may know herself to be
deeply and fully loved by the doglike God.

Contents

Preface
To the New Edition

This book is about a black lab named Cluny. As I write, her ashes sit in a cloth bag on my desk. When the family gathers next, we will scatter her ashes along the Kadunce River, near her favorite hike, alongside a ruddy shelf the river slides around.

Cluny died before her twelfth birthday. As we drove to the vet, she rested her head in my lap and looked into my tear-streaked face. I could tell she wanted to comfort me, but couldn't.

Oh, yes, there are and will be other dogs. Cluny helped train in Lucy for a year before she died. (Lucy, who, after a great victory, prefers the moniker, "She Who Trees Bears.") But Cluny was one of those rare dogs who you know, even as they live at your expense, is one in a million, the dog of a lifetime.

When I first wrote this account of Cluny and some of what she had taught me about God, I had experienced some sadness, some loss, some loneliness. On one low day, I had realized that even at those times when I wasn't so sure that God wanted to hear from me, I always knew that Cluny would bounce to meet me, jumping and wagging her joy to the world. And so, over the next couple years, I had taken time to meditate on what my spirituality would be like if I believed that God loved me even half as much as my dear Cluny. And this is the volume that I produced.

In the years since I first wrote *Dogspell,* my life took a radical turn. Most of us who are pastors and teachers, who assure others that they won't be asked to shoulder something they can't bear, and remind them that "underneath are the everlasting arms," wonder how we would manage if we met with the unimaginable. Would we really find our words to be true? Would we find God to be as faithful as our dogs?

When my husband of nearly thirty years divorced me to marry a woman whom I considered a close friend, I could not imagine how I would continue to live. Trust, security, financial freedom, future plans, children's sense of belonging: All seemed to be replaced by betrayal, confusion, anxiety, and rage.

Through all the unfaithfulness, Cluny was faithful. But more important, Cluny as a metaphor for God pointed to the truth of the faithfulness of God. I hit bottom, and the bottom held. God was there, as dog was. Underneath I was held by the "everlasting paws."

And so I offer this new edition of *Dogspell*, convinced of its crucial relevance to spiritual seekers today. So many have had their trust shattered, or have learned of a God who loves only on good hair days. The experience many of us have had with the love of dog points to a God whose love is greater, not only than those who let us down, but even than the love of dog.

As I work with students, faculty, parishioners, neighbors, I meet so many people whose idea of God is warped by those in religious authority who used an arbitrary God to frighten followers into good behavior. I want to invite those people to explore the God whom they've experienced in the wag of a great tail, the nudge of a soft wet tongue.

Mary Ellen Ashcroft
January 14, 2008

Acknowledgments

I am grateful for the dogged faithfulness and winsome wisdom of some wonderful soul mates: Suzanne Sherman, Letha Wilson-Barnard, Peg Thompson, and Jo Bailey Wells. I am also thankful for the fortitude, wisdom and humor of my children and their partners: Susannah and Chris, Stephen and Anna, Andrew and Jennye. I feel blessed to have had a dog like Cluny for the years I had her; and also to have her successors, Lucy and Torrie.

Introduction

Sadness pushed me to write this dogmatic theology. My eldest went a thousand miles away to college, and despite a loving family, supportive friends, and a great job, I felt down in the whisker. One evening, I went into the kitchen and our two-year-old black lab greeted me warmly. Instead of patting and pushing past her, "Down, Cluny, down!" I sat on the floor. She pushed her chest against mine to get a little closer and then flopped down next to me, head in my lap, tip of her tail wagging.

What is so deeply comforting, I wondered, about the love of dog? Over the next few months, I realized the truth: Despite years of prayer, religious seeking, theological training, and church involvement, I believed more fully in the steadfast love and faithfulness of dog than of God.

About this time, a friend looked up from her dog's greeting and asked me: "Is there any religion—has there ever been one—that speaks of a God who loves us as much as a dog?" Theologians have long argued that God must be the greatest being we can imagine. Anselm of Canterbury, for instance, argued that God must be "That than which no greater thing can be thought."[1] But in my spiritual life, I expect less loving response, nurture, and welcome from God than I do from dog. And I'm not the only one: "If I thought that God loved me as much as my dog," a student said to me, 'it would change everything. I wouldn't be looking for love in all the wrong places." Many of us have fashioned or accepted a God smaller, meaner, more petty than our dogs.

Central to human longing, I believe, is the desire to be met and welcomed, to be deeply loved. The heart of faith beats with God's (doglike) greeting presence. From the beginning, God has longed to w-a-l-k with us in the garden, but organized religion has often worked to block God's welcoming movement—forcing people to scale and contort, hurdle and crawl to get anywhere near God.

"Are you writing anything at the moment?" people ask me. When I've answered, "Well, a sort of dog theology . . . ," I've gotten raised eyebrows and shocked glances, quickly papered over with, "Interesting." "I wondered what I could learn about God from thinking about dog," I say, trying to explain that I'm exploring a metaphor of God as dog.

Yet reflecting on the doggishness of God is not as odd as it sounds, since we cannot talk about God without metaphor. Metaphors shed light on the abstract (helping us to see in new ways), but they are also supposed to shock us. When Jesus used metaphors for himself in the Gospels, his listeners often responded in surprise or even disgust. The Bible uses an enormous range of metaphors—like eagle, mother hen, rock, father—all of which shed different light on the nature of (and our experience of) God. A good metaphor should make us squirm a bit as it highlights some aspect of God that has been neglected or underemphasized.

Stopping to consider it, most people understand that any metaphor has helpful aspects, and others that are not so beneficial—the "is" and "is not." In other words, metaphors function to shed light on one thing by comparing it to another, but parts of the comparison break down. Although the biblical metaphor "God is my rock" tells us something about God's solid steadfastness (the "is"), we don't assume that we can do some sort of geological sampling on God to find out whether God is basalt (the "is not").

The "is" and "is not" is true for *all* metaphors. British writer Dorothy L. Sayers says this about the metaphor of God the Father:

> Nor (unless we are very stupid indeed) do we go on
> to deduce from the analogy that we are to imagine

God as being a cruel, careless or injudicious father such as we may see from time to time in daily life; still less, that *all* the activities of a human father may be attributed to God, such as earning money for the support of the family or demanding the first use of the bathroom in the morning.[2]

Thinking of a metaphor as a drawing that overlaps the abstract may be helpful. Draw a rock and the sketch overlaps God in some ways, but not in others. A dog drawing may overlap particular traits of God, but not others; a picture of a father suggests certain truths about what God is like, but not all. Because God is God and because human language is limited, no one outline could ever match completely; no metaphor tells all. If it did, it would cease to be a metaphor and perhaps cease to be useful in aiding our understanding of God. (Some would argue that this has happened with a metaphor like God the Father or an analogy like being "born again.")

Some of our most strongly held but dimly understood metaphors are directional ones, which tell us that down is bad and up is good. These probably find their roots in Platonic ideas that flesh and earth are bad, that the wholly spiritual is good. In my pursuit of a dog theology, I try to challenge these directional metaphors, too.

At different stages in our lives, one metaphor may elucidate God more fully than others. And although some metaphors may not be helpful for me in my spiritual life right now, I'm not about to abandon them. I may not find "king" the most enlightening of metaphors for God because I meet so little royalty nowadays (perhaps it's my neighborhood?), but I keep that metaphor within my store so that it can enrich and challenge me, later if not now.

When we overuse one metaphor or one set of metaphors, we are in fact leaning into heresy. Sovereign metaphors for God, for instance, emphasizing kingship, thrones, majesty, and judgment may be true. But overused, they become not only irrelevant (when did you last, in your daily life, bow before a throne?), they become heretical, as they give an incomplete (and therefore false) picture of what God is like. Similarly, military metaphors for the Christian life may be fine used sparingly, but overused these "fight" and "war" metaphors become unhelpful, pushing us to think of others as the enemy or putting us on the defensive. Still, we certainly need many metaphors to even begin to understand someone as great and wonderful as God.

Moreover, certain metaphors will better aid understanding and worship for different individuals. Some childhood abuse victims struggle with the metaphor of God as father, but the most obvious solution—God as mother—may be unhelpful to women whose mothers were frustrated by images of womanhood in the fifties.

Similarly, those who were ravaged by dogs may not find *Dogspell* a breath of fresh air. But for many, I hope, my whimsical exploration will shed light on God's greeting, God's choice of identification, God's steadfast love and faithfulness.

Everyone's heard about the agnostic dyslexic who wondered, "Is there a dog?" I'm here to testify that, yes, there is a dog, who is alive and well and eager to greet you. I hope in this book to justify the ways of dog to humankind. Let's face it, for dog's sake: One of our big problems is that no one has seen dog. I hope that *Dogspell* will help us all "To know the love of [dog] which passeth all understanding" (John 14:27 KJV).

Dog Stories

Cluny really loves me. She loves to be with me. Deposit your check at the bank? Love it. When I'm driving, she puts her head on my shoulder. Clean out the basement? Why not? If I'm in the dining room, Cluny gets a mouthful of food and puts it next to my chair so that she can be near me while she eats. "If that's where you are, that's where I want to be," says Cluny.

If I'm sad, Cluny comforts me. If I feel down in the whisker, she licks my face and sits her ninety pounds on my lap. Yes, Cluny loves me.

When I was young, I read and reread dog stories—*Old Yeller, Sounder, Savage Sam, Where the Red Fern Grows, Lassie Come Home, The Incredible Journey.* The mound of soggy Kleenexes by my bed grew. Swimming raging rivers, facing snakes or cougars, laboring over mountain passes, dog searches for her beloved.

And the climax? She yelps her hello, the owner hears, disbelief swallowed in joy. Then the meeting: knocked over by love, flattened by greeting, wagging tail, licked face. Or sometimes the death of dog for the owner. To what lengths will a dog go just to be with the beloved?

I know dog loves me. I rest secure in the faithfulness of dog; I know dog's welcome is assured. Okay, I'm not sure about her scaling mountain passes or facing rattlers, but I know she likes me and will give me a warm welcome when I come home.

I open the kitchen door (I've been gone almost an hour), and I'm overwhelmed by jumping, licking, wagging, whining: "Where were you? I missed you! Why were you gone so long?" Cluny's ninety pounds join the wag. "Love you, love you, love you. . . ."

What if I believed that God loved, welcomed, longed to greet me as much as dog? A loving God? Of course, I believe it; I say the Nicene Creed Sunday by Sunday.

But I confess that I don't believe in a God who yearns to meet me as I long to be met.

Theologians have (somehow) missed this remarkable truth: Christianity is the ultimate dog story. The incredible journey starts with God whelped as a pup in Bethlehem. In Galilee, he walks with people (healing, of course) or sits with them, wagging, nuzzling. And finally the desperate rescue attempt—scaling mountains, fording streams, and dying in his efforts. To what lengths will God go to be with the beloved?

God Tumbles to Be with Us

I knew a family whose dog stayed upstairs, except when the doorbell rang. Then Rex raced across the carpeted landing and down the stairs in welcome. When they took up the carpet and polished the floors, Rex couldn't get used to it. In the joy of his doggish greeting, he would race across the landing and tumble head over tail down the whole flight to welcome them.

Caution, prudence, careful forethought are not big dog traits. Enthusiasm, refusing to take no for an answer, careening down stairs in welcome—that's what dog is like.

God makes a world and seeks a world, speaking, calling, holding out loving hands. God longs to w-a-l-k with us in the cool of the day. In each prophet, sage, visitation: Dog searches, sniffs.

Like God, Cluny forgets she's huge—that she has a big tail and enormous paws. In her desire to love you, she wants to climb into your lap. Like Cluny, God became lap God, compressed in multiple cell form, squeezed into the smallest place, growing in Mary's womb. Not watching from a distance, but closer than close, within and around—Emmanuel.

God sits on the top step, watching, wagging. God scrambles down, setting up tent with flesh and blood—God-with-us.

Doggish Greetings and Our Desire to Be Met

(Dog Is Love; Love Is of Dog)

"Stay," I say to Cluny when I walk across the street to talk to my neighbor. "Good dog," I say picking up her leash, and she throws herself at me. "Cluny, I know you love me. I know you've missed me. Really, this is too much. I've been gone less than a minute. Let's be reasonable."

Reasonable, schmeasonable. Dogs don't do calculated, strategic, or careful.

They want to jump up on almost everyone. I hired a man from a local treatment program to help me clean carpets. Clearly life had been hard on him. He had few teeth, smelled of tobacco and sweat, hadn't bathed or changed for some time. I opened the door for him, and Cluny lunged at him, licking his face. He dropped onto his knees as Cluny covered him with kisses, wagging and twisting with joy. He looked up at me through tears. "I can't tell you how I miss my dog. I had to leave her in Texas."

Cluny, we say, is big on hellos. She doesn't like good-byes. When any member of the family gets a suitcase out, she curls around it, looking mournful.

Doglike, God knows that, more than anything, we want to be met. Face-to-face, flesh-to-flesh greetings form the heart of human longing and the center of Christian spirituality. The church's great festivals reflect this: God (in the Incarnation) moves to meet us on our own turf; Easter is the meeting beyond all hope; at Pentecost that greeting becomes daily experience. God is one big welcome in the Trinity, endlessly loving, creating, greeting.

Flesh and blood meetings are the warp and woof of the biblical stories, where God doggedly sniffs out David in the fields, barks up the right tree at Zacchaeus. And the sacraments: In Baptism, God welcomes; in the Eucharist, God meets and feeds. The wholly spiritual, the completely fleshly: Neither will do. We crave the intermingling of flesh and spirit that is God—God the greeter, waiting doglike, ears twitching for the sound of the key in the door.

Dog sprawls on the kitchen floor, gently snoozing. Her ears twitch, because she knows they'll be here soon. The slightest sound and she's up, barking, yes, but more to warm her voice for the greeting, to get her tail in gear for the big wag.

Our ears strain for this greeting, the yelp of recognition that echoes beyond hope. Our hankering to meet God lives in all our embraces. To w-a-l-k with God in the cool of the day.

Longing

A dog named Hachiko met his owner, a Tokyo professor, off his subway train each evening. For nine years after his master's death, Hachiko made his way to the station and waited. Another dog, Greyfriars Bobby, sat by his master's Edinburgh grave for fourteen years.

Bronze statues in Tokyo and Edinburgh immortalize the desire, the faithful longing of these dogs. That deep desire for the beloved—what does it remind me of? I remember . . . a black and white photo exhibition.

A black and white photo catches the same hunger, freezes it for all time in a mother's eyes. Taken at the end of World War II, the picture shows a woman, standing on a European train platform, searching the faces of soldiers finally home.

Her face takes my breath away.

He is no longer a child, she reminds herself, touching her pocket, where she keeps his photograph. War. Perhaps he's been horribly disfigured. For a moment, all she remembers of him is the feeling of moving his little hand through the sleeve of a red baby sweater. "Maybe his mind is gone and he won't know me. . . . Maybe he's already gone past me. I will have to search for him. . . . Will I know him?"

The desperate expectation in her eyes mirrors all deeply held desires, all stark abandonment. Surely she could not endure the white heat of this anguish for more than a few minutes.

And yet she has. When the photographer snapped this picture, her longing, her hoping against hope, may have lasted years. And when will it end? The last soldier steps off the train, and she tugs on the guard's arm. "Where are the others? My son should be here. . . ." her voice shakes with the delirium, the nausea of waiting forever.

Her face makes me dizzy, holding as it does the human experience of longing: consuming tenderness washed over by tides of war, disease, death. She cannot forget that she has borne and suckled, that her life is woven into his. Would she go back and undo this? Suffocate Christopher at birth to sidestep the anguish? She cannot forget, cannot exorcise herself of love.

The dog sits—at the train station looking for her master, in the cemetery searching every face.

The Meeting

And still she stands—this woman, bent slightly in her eagerness, her face burning with desire—him? No. Him? No. Him? No, no . . . but the earlobe flattening lightly against the cheek, the nostril slightly pointed. . . .

That split second. An earthquake roars and the concrete opens in front of her. Trees freeze, drop their leaves, and burst into blossom. The sun dies in the sky, and a new young sun leaps up. The constellations wheel; the Southern Cross shoves the Big Dipper out of the way for this meeting.

Tears, hugging, kissing, names murmured, laughter, eyes devouring, jumping, licking, tails wagging—this moment of meeting. Like Mary Magdalene in the garden: "I can't even pull my wearied eyes across his body, can't feel his cold flesh because they've taken the body, and where is it? What are they doing with it? Where have you put him?" she mumbles through tears beyond tears. And there he is, dearly remembered jawbone running to his ear and lines at the side of his eyes. Mary, Rabboni, Christopher, Mama, Lassie . . . the name flashes, snapping into place what had come disjointed, setting and healing the compound, searing fracture, the father hugs the swine-smelling son, lifting him off his feet in his joy.

This encounter, whispered in all our joys, beats in the heart of humanity, in myths across time and space. The old folktales reverberate with meetings and wondrous discoveries. Welcome the smelly bag lady, and she may turn out to be a princess, goddess, or angel. Innkeeping folks invite Mary and Joseph to bed down for a night, and look what happens!

Hospitality—the unboundaried heart—means that anything could happen: God will meet us in the most unlikely guises. "A funny smell over here," says Cluny as she sniffs the woman sitting next to the fireplace. "Smells like Glory to me." Sure enough, she's an angel unaware (Heb 13:2).

Slam the door in someone's face, be mean to a visitor, and you're asking for trouble, declare the old stories. *Cinderella* and *Sleeping Beauty* recount hospitality gone wrong. You can't judge, remember, by clothes. This foundling, this orphan, this alien probably has blue blood. Relegate her to the cinders or try to kill her, lord it over her because of your greater wealth or better connections, and you'll be in trouble. The stranger acts as a prophet, showing the true mettle of hosts by their welcome of guests. In Dante's *Inferno*, bad hosts find their eternal torture near hell's bottom.

When we brought the tabby kitten home, Cluny bounced up to Wilbur, who arched and spat. Cluny stepped back, stunned. She sat and stared for ten minutes at the tiny face and then dropped down and started sliding toward the kitten. Wilbur spat and batted Cluny's nose. Over the next few days, Cluny spent hours sitting as close as she could to Wilbur. If the kitten sat, Cluny sat; if the kitten reclined, Cluny was prone, eyes fastened on the new family member's face. God-like, Cluny was desperate to welcome Wilbur.

Dog welcomes and greets all and sundry, whether they are wearing cat fur, polyester or silk, drinking cream, Folgers or Ethiopian dark roast. Like dog, God ushers us straight into the living room and invites us to make ourselves at home. The waiting room, the line at immigration, the hospital lounge, the FBI checkpoint—delay tactics to show who's in charge—these are wagged away by a God who knows you can't judge by a credit rating, by someone's past—and a lick across the glasses might help.

The great moment in dog stories is the one where dog hears human, human hears dog. What's that sound, that whine, that bark? It's impossible! Open the door, and it's true—beyond all expectation they've conquered danger. Their paws ache, but it's all right! Lassie leaps over the fence.

3

Afraid to Meet Dog

(Your Sins Have Made a Separation between You and Your Dog)

Thresholds between here and there, now and then, heaven and earth: These are the fissures in our lives, where for a moment the cosmic bubbles out, steams its heady smell. In the split second before the crevasse snaps shut, if we pay attention, we might taste what we most deeply desire, might tingle with a split-second longing for embrace.

Cracks of greeting open wherever meetings happen, like the road outside the sharecroppers' house in *Sounder*, when the old three-legged coon dog hears his crippled master returning after years in prison:

> Suddenly the voice of the great coon hound broke
> the sultry August deadness. The dog dashed along

the road, leaving three-pointed clouds of red dust to settle back to earth behind him. The mighty voice rolled out upon the valley, each flutelike bark echoing from slope to slope.

Sounder was a young dog again. His voice was the same mellow sound that had ridden the November breeze from the lowlands to the hills. The boy and his mother looked at each other.

Sounder's master had come home.[3]

The farm road, that European train platform, docks with ticker tape and flower petals, the driveway with car doors thrown open and the family (two- and four-footed members) running down the steps, even airports: All are holy ground. Families welcome new members, having fingered their pictures for months. Grandparents meet their youngest grandchild, and joy explodes in waving arms, silly faces.

I stand at the airport, watching passengers emerge from their flights. I search their eyes: the weary businessman, laptop slung nonchalantly over his shoulder; an older couple, looking around to make sure the other is there; the student, pushing her hair back, holding her Penguin edition of some obscure novel.

Flung headlong across time and space, they glance at us earthbound in the waiting area, and I can see the flicker—if only, if only, if only—and then the cover-up: "I didn't expect anyone to meet me, of course; I travel too much."

What is that split second of expectation if not one shore of the God-shaped hole within each of us? Traipsing home prodigal-like from Tulsa or Paris, we long for the delighted eyes of a father, making a fool of himself as he careens toward us—robes flying behind him as he runs—desperate to greet his beloved.

Stitching, Madly Stitching

Frequent disappointment miles have dulled us: No longer naked, no longer ashamed, we step from air to earth—world explorers who know how to keep ourselves covered. "Bye. Thanks for flying with us." A commercial greeting must do. Forget the cosmic welcome.

Our desolation goes back eons. After all, what was the garden but soft green light, bird sounds, flowers, and an intimate w-a-l-k with God in the cool of the day? The fault lines of the fall, the huge cracks in our world are outward and visible signs of the deep cracks in our souls.

Searching the garden is God: Where are you? Dog sniffs them out. There they are, crouched, distracted, pathetically stitching fig leaves, pricking their fingers and dying, always dying. This is sin: the stitching, frantic pulling together of fig leaves, covering self—with success, sex appeal, status—so that grace can find no chink. "What do you want?" Adam heaves a stick at dog. "Is it that hard to see we're naked?" he asks Eve.

Naked. God freezes: "Who told you that you were naked?"

Not notice your nakedness? Exposure is more than flesh and blood can bear; it reruns through our nightmares, the dreamer addressing a large audience and suddenly realizing her nakedness.

Scrambling out of the garden, Adam and Eve shed intimacy and meeting (naked and not ashamed) for life on the superficial film of the bubble. She looks in the mirror: "Lipstick smeared? Face on? Should I wear the knee-length fig leaf?" Meanwhile, Adam hunkers down there in the garden, stitching himself up some honor. He wonders: "Do my muscles show better in the sleeveless?" We crouch, making our going-away outfits, while God calls. Sewing, you might prick your finger and know your flesh to be the same God wears.

Before they leave the garden, God clothes Adam and Eve. A long-standing enemy of the fashion industry, God only knows they'll need all the skins they can get to have their backsides covered in this brave new world, where people are looking out for number one and loneliness is a never-ending agony. And it's true: You can't live naked outside the garden. Covering nakedness becomes an act of charity.

"How do I look?" she wonders, tugging the skin that those cosmic hands gently tucked over her shoulder and around her arm, checking that it shows just the right amount of leg, while the sun sets on her Eve.

God Is There to Meet the Plane

What if a miracle happened at the gate? The pilot announces final approach: "We are now approaching the Twin Cities of Minneapolis, St. Paul. The temperature is 62; looks like a very pleasant evening. On behalf of our whole crew and Northwest Airlines, we thank you for flying with us. And by the way, as a special treat this evening, God will be meeting you off this flight."

I'm a person of faith, but they'd have to pull me off that plane. Like Eve, like Adam, I'd hide beneath the seat, see if I could fit my bulk into one of the overhead bins. Sure I want to be met, but not by God—not in these clothes, with this luggage, in this frame of mind. . . .

Why am I terrified to meet God? So carefully clothed myself, I have covered God in the dress of those who demanded my best behavior—teachers, principals, ministers. I have covered God's naked joy with my dad's suit, my mom's "Sunday best," the priest's black cassock. Our understanding of God, they say, has roots entangled in childhood authority figures, beyond the reach of our theology. The God I knew as a child was critical, detached, touchy. I had to be careful because he was looking down on me and might turn, any second, into a cold and cruel judge. Over the years, I have fashioned a god I want to keep my distance from.

The flight attendant and captain lean over me, struggling to pull away my sewing kit. "Sorry, Ma'am, you must get off the plane; we're preparing for another flight. No, you can't go to Tampa without a ticket. You must get off." I clutch my Penguin edition of *The Oddessy* like a shield before me. I prepare my laptop as a sword. I don the helmet of ennui—how boring, really, all these flights. I rush to catch a taxi.

What if I believed God was half as loving as dog? I imagine coming down the ramp, through the glass door. I'd be shoving a bit at the man in front of me, standing on tiptoes to see her glossy black head. She'd catch a whiff of me and bark my name, and hurl herself at me, knocking me off my feet. Who cares about the expensive laptop, the new Penguin edition? Throw your hat away! There in public, at the airport, people stepping over and around me, she'd lick my face and I'd be shouting, "Yes! I love you! I'm so happy to see you too!"

But it's embarrassing. I don't want a God who runs joyfully to greet me, one who cannot contain exuberance, who shouts and dances the pleasure of meeting. That's okay in dogs and babies, for heaven's sake. God shouldn't be so enthusiastic, nor should God be so vulnerable to pain. I've clothed myself so that the hurt of not being met cannot touch me. Why can't God stay properly covered?

Dog Tears Off Her Bandanna

(Veiled in Flesh the Doghead See)

Having worked so hard on our own outfits, we try to clothe God. No shirt, no shoes, no service, we say. God-dressing sounds difficult—harder even than clothing Cluny. But God-dressing is the easiest thing there is; for many, it's a compulsive hobby.

God deserves the best-dressed celebrity award, and my outfits wouldn't even place. The church has robed God in fine marble, gilt, marvelous mosaic. Let God be anything but naked. Yes, I want that cloth there, gracefully, gently flowing. Thank you, sculptors, for helping God where God could not help God's self. Just as I have protected myself from the enthusiastic greeting of God, artists daub away to cover God's bare flesh and unprotected love.

We've tried putting a bandanna on Cluny—just the thing for the well-dressed dog. She chews it off. For a snow-shoeing venture, we put little black fleece boots on her, with Velcro straps. She lost three in one afternoon. Sat down and munched them off. If we took Cluny to a groomer, I suspect she'd pull out the bow and find some mud.

Maybe God, like dog, can't keep anything on, not even my kindly contributed business suits, navy pumps, chasubles. The message must have gotten lost that God should sport Sunday best or dress for success.

God stripped off finery and appeared—my God, how embarrassing—naked as the day he was born. God rips off medals of rank, puts aside titles, special honors, particular talents, and faces us in his birthday suit. Veiled in flesh the Godhead see; hail the incarnate deity. The angel and Mary greet each other, the Incarnation begins, and soon things heavenly and earthly are gathered into one: one in the naked flesh and folds of God.

When the Gospel was first preached, Romans laughed at the idea of a God become flesh. Oh, sure, a god might have a little fling with a mortal woman and then disappear to better realms, but no real mixing, please. You know your side of the tracks, the gods know theirs. God become flesh—hilarious!

Instead of laughing, we've done a sleight of hand to turn the celebration of the Incarnation—presto chango—into Christmas. Into the hat we stuff a fleshly God; out pops tinsel, wrapping paper, photos of children with starry eyes. The incantation? Hocus-pocus backwards—no, this is not my body, not my blood, God's very flesh tucked up my sleeve.

Dig under stockings, credit card bills, Christmas concert programs. Pull off layers of carols, drifts of snow, a gingerbread house recipe and—oh, my God! What is it? A baby! Not a silent, glow-in-the-dark symbol of benign blessing on farm animals. The merconium, the squalling cries, the desperate need for warm breast, for eyes to search his: God is naked and not ashamed.

The feast of the Incarnation is the time to celebrate God weak, a day to dance to the descending scales of God's throwing off omniscience and omnipotence. We skirt past this powerful little pile of cast-off clothing. Like the magazine reflection of a starving boy's eyes, the bruises of an abused girl on the news—our eyes cannot adjust to this. We do not want this God, whose glory is so dim we strain to see it.

Our little pile of clothes is nothing compared to God's, but we cling to it. We pull our fig leaves, our animal skins, around us, and we wish that God Almighty had the good sense to do the same. We toss him the towel of our Christmas celebrations for a cover-up.

Pile over him the Christmas tree skirt, the Christmas card list, the invitation to a Christmas party. His cries are almost suffocated. Turn on somebody's Christmas CD: I don't care whose. I don't want a God who becomes flesh.

As we cover God with Christmas, we carefully bury the jewel of Christian spirituality—God's choice of Incarnation, of identification with pain, humanity, flesh. Early Christmas hymns sing of Incarnation; most Victorian ones hum harps of gold.

A dog in a manger full of hay, according to one of Aesop's fables, snarled at an ox who came to eat, and the phrase "dog in the manger" epitomizes meanness: "I don't want it, and I don't want you to have it either." Incarnation, true dog in the manger, says the opposite: "I would go to any length to give myself and all I have to you."

The true Christmas story scares us spitless. God sets a precedent; skins to infiltrate, identify. Then the ultimate horror story: He strips even the dusty garments of human mortality for his last act, his cross-dressing.

If God undressed, we might have to join him— remove our self-sufficiency suits, pull off our health and wellness sweats, our latest designer outfits. The word was made flesh and dwelt among us—God with us, closer than close. Get naked: That is the path of God.

Dog Slides Down the Slippery Slope
(Dog with Us)

Cluny: Dog with me. When I write, she curls around my chair. I get up to put some laundry in, and she walks by my side down to the laundry room and sits. Then she walks back upstairs with me. If I am sad, she licks my tears. When I'm happy, she dances with me. Where love is, where pain is, where death is, where joy is—Dog is there. Cluny leaps off the dock into the water, eager to rescue or romp with whomever has dived in. Down and out—it seems—is the only way to go.

God invites us there—down and out—and some religion follows the movement of God: The Salvation Army was founded to welcome outcasts; the Taize community in France has become a reconciling place for all seekers. In a Presbyterian church I once attended, the neatly suited ushers nearly broke their necks to welcome a barefooted, dungareed young man and bring him into the heart of the worship.

But often religion issues another invitation—lift and separate—moving God away, out of reach, yours only if you're very, very good. Will you sign the pledge, be celibate, accept Jesus Christ as your personal lord and savior, promise to have a quiet time daily, donate large sums to the poor?

God leaps over dividing walls, scratches at doors, pulls away fallen branches. Dad belts, hollering, down the drive, knocking down his son in his exuberance. The veil of the temple was torn in two from top to bottom for easy access to God. The church has done its best to sew these huge flaps back together so that people are kept from God.

You can talk to dogs 'til you're blue in the face, asking them to conform to certain standards, put a paw print on the line showing they will never jump, lick, or wag, but it doesn't help. They see through the highfalutin' stuff to what really counts—doing the whole body wag and welcoming everyone.

The slippery slope: Fear-mongering religious leaders tell us that's where we are, teetering at the top, and if we aren't careful, we'll end up at the bottom with sinners. And it's true: The slippery slope (although God's terrain of choice) is a terrible location in clerical garb or a fancy suit. Pushing a marble statue (or your pulpit) up a slippery slope is no fun. Religious types often stay on top, shouting instructions, throwing down tracts (or, even more dangerous, theological tomes). If you believe cleanliness is next to godliness, eschew slippery slopes.

If you want to get down and dirty (like God), then go for the slippery slope. God topples to greet Levi (licking hands soiled by filthy lucre), touches lepers, unclean women, the dead. (Please, God, could you keep your paws out of the mud? We'd prefer you to stand majestic up, up, up there.) God tumbles into place at Zacchaeus's table, finds himself at muddy banquets, on the street.

St. Francis, Dorothy Day, Oscar Romero, Mother Teresa (and countless others whose names we've never heard) see the down-and-outness of God. They peel power, prestige, respectable religion, and slide, snowboarding, down, down. The greetings at the bottom of the slippery slope leave muddy footprints, full of exceeding glory.

God could have chosen distance: contemplating from a detached, divine reverie, creating inanimate objects and slinging them around the universe. God could just be, spinning ever further from a suffering world. God could be masked with the impenetrable, passive face of a plaster Buddha, gazing beyond pain. When I confront terrible pain, I wish I had that untouched face as my ideal so I could distance myself from the dust, flesh, and torment of the human condition.

What could be less doglike than a statue of Buddha? Sit. Stay. Look impassive. Don't wag your tail. I said, sit. Stay. Less enthusiasm please, and more sophistication. Try to be mysterious and distant.

No, the face of God is spun with joy, drawn by pain, creased with greeting. God avoids sanctuaries of esoteric understanding, wandering instead into the mud of identification, the spit and dirt of costly involvement. In flesh we endure heat, cold, toothache; in flesh we fear the rapist, the cancer. God could not be God-with-us without flesh. The spit of God mixed with the dirt of Galilee makes a healing paste.

The descent of God was headlong. Like a child scraping her knee, an elderly man slipping on ice, a soldier picked off by a sniper, a sparrow hitting a window—God falls. The stroke victim weeps as he tries to remember, the quadriplegic contemplates suicide, realizing he will not move again, the old woman twists as she sees herself victim to a broken hip. God has chosen to fall—to limit mental and physical powers in the Incarnation. What does it mean to have a God who falls?

Dog Rolls in Something

(Dog So Loved the World)

Dogs are not otherworldly or hyperspiritual. I know Cluny is there by her smell, her tongue, her lean, her tail beating against my leg. Dogs are pretty happy being flesh and blood, and so is God. All our hiding, our God-dressing, none of it works: God strips divine strength, becomes down-and-out, and chooses the most unlikely place from which to seek us—flesh.

This is the essence of God, right up to the End Time Gala portrayed in Revelation. Trumpets blast, hordes of characters freeze (Cecil B. DeMille to the 100th power, the opening of the Olympic games to the 1,000th) for a word from the Almighty, and what is it? Fanfare, drum roll, the envelope, please: "Behold, the dwelling of God is with mortals" (Rev 21:3, KJV). I'm sorry—could we be a teensy bit more profound? You're telling me that the climax of the epic, the moral of the story, is that God wants me to scoot over on the couch so that there's room for God to sit with me, a mere mortal?

No angel hand almost, almost touching, leaving a space of antiseptic mystery in between. Study with a microscope, if you like, the inches Botticelli painted in his Annunciation: The Virgin bends, stunned by her flesh in the presence of eternal mystery. Extending fingers, the angel speaks: Wait, listen. And in that space anything might happen, as long as it happens ethereally, without touching.

How about an annunciation in the style of the flesh-God? Clutching each other, dancing the tango, they romp out of the house, frolicking through market and countryside, leapfrogging. Not the celebration of "best woman's curtsey of all time," the Annunciation stands instead as Mary's boisterous *yes* to advent/adventure, to inexplicable knowing of God, to knitting within herself a body for one loved but strange. She is holy like we all should be—wholly alive and wholly met by God. Flesh, yes, but no veiling here, no artful annunciations; instead, that primal element of the universe, women's flesh. Mary sings a song of woman's blessed flesh, blessed indeed by God's choice of flesh. In the Annunciation, God enunciates the word most clearly, speaking in bone and sinew.

The gravity, the trauma—oh, my God—and another, and another, jamming, pressing, can't breathe—and into the birth canal, the tightest spot God will ever be in. Pushed, squeezed, stuck. And then the miracle: God slips into the world—bloody, slimy, squalling.

Birth, like death, is bloody. Staring into her dead son's face, nothing could be further from virgin. Mary's love like hunger: Sweat and muscle of man, yet every age present as his life sighs away, and she strokes, traces every bone, freckle, and joint, imprinting them on her very self. Face contorted by pain, eyes glazed, he is animal. In a true Pieta—never yet painted or sculpted—flesh meets flesh.

Destroy all the paintings; burn them as heretics, testifying as they do to a false faith, one emptied of flesh, human agency, emotion. Can the passion be the passion emptied of pain and love? Give me paintings of Mary, scared and excited, dripping milk and in rapture at her babe. Give me a Pieta where she is furious, devastated.

I reach out to touch Jesus, and my hand goes right through him—he is the ghost of Good Friday past. We claim his saving blood, but not his limbic life. Like mother, like son: The church has made them both haunts, ghosts. It is the invasion of the body snatchers, the church frantically pulling veils (nice suits, habits, chasubles) over the centrality of God's choice. Will you renounce? Will you sign the pledge?

What God has joined together—flesh and spirit—let no one pull asunder. We're not so sure about this flesh/spirit concoction—though both were blended in the garden (and we occasionally see them in a good partnership, a happy parent-child relationship, a great friendship)—we try to remove all flesh or all spirit. All flesh over here: centerfold layouts, pornography, steamy novels—it's okay, simply pleasures of the flesh. Over here, spiritual only, please: celibacy, fasting, asceticism, legalism. The extraordinary alloy of flesh and spirit, an alloy perfected in the person of Jesus is too exotic for our taste.

The Incarnation is about taking one part God and one part flesh and pureeing them, first for nine months, and then for thirty-three years. Yes, and from that point on, the recipe holds, tested as it was in those best of all possible kitchens. Our life of faith is frapped, not layered.

God emptied God of divine prerogative to become flesh, and much religion has worked tirelessly for two millennia to reverse that process, unpicking all those frapped molecules that are such an extraordinary blend of spirit and flesh. Under a microscope—oops, here's a little more flesh, let's get it out of here.

God must have known the downside of flesh before climbing into it: Flesh gets sick, feels pain, demands food, longs for pleasure, tingles with goose bumps. Flesh dies.

God permeated flesh, and flesh permeated God with weakness, hunger, temptation, and death.

In the woods, Cluny finds a dead squirrel; by the lake she smells rotting trout and rolls herself right into it, shoulder, neck, head, rolling and rolling. She bounces toward me, eyes filled with joy, "Guess what I found? You'll never believe it! Can you smell?" My response is less than enthusiastic, "Yuk, you wretched animal. Bath for you." I wish her instinctual urges to relay scent messages to the wolf pack had been domesticated out of her. Why would anyone roll in something dead?

Cleanliness is nowhere near godliness, for dog or God. Keeping paws clean, standing back and not getting messy—that's not the way of God. No, dog goes straight in and rolls in it, no matter how gross. In the Incarnation, especially in the crucifixion, God rolls in flesh, covers self—shoulders, neck and head—with the smell of death.

Dog Puts Together a Party List
(The Call of Dog)

Cluny is a retriever. If I throw a ball into the lake, she swims to fetch it. She can't help retrieving; it's in her blood. I throw a stick and Cluny doesn't shake her head in disgust: "What's so special about this particular stick? You throw it away and then ask me to run after it? What's it worth to you to get this stick back?"

Toe in, toe out—we'd reel off questions before taking the plunge—Cluny's already back with the stick. Like dog, God retrieves—instinctually pulling people from brush or water—and prances back delighted with the mouthful.

Let's face it. Cluny is foolish, ridiculous in her use of time, indiscreet in her affectional preference.

Cluny jumps up on a Brooks Brothers suit or a spiked leather jacket. Skin brown, pink, pierced, tattooed—

doesn't matter. Nicodemus and the religious establishment, harlots and tax collectors: She leaps on them all. She licks collaborators with the Roman regime. She springs onto homosexuals, nuns, grunge-look teens. She's never met a person she wouldn't welcome to her party.

"Dogs! Why can't they stay down?" mutters the businessman, bending to wipe his muddy suit cuff. Cluny licks his face. Ninety-nine greet her warmly, but she knows there's another, and off she goes, tail up, nose down, searching for someone who needs retrieving, who longs (she assumes) for her greeting.

Read the Bible and what do you find? God, like dog, is foolhardy, shortsighted, color-blind.

The Foolishness of God

God's choices—you must admit—are ill-considered, absurdly unstrategic, downright irrational. If he'd kept his wits about him—not discarding his omniscience when he needed it most—God could have hit the ground running, birthed as emperor or king, at least to wealth. A wise and judicious God—one to the manor born—would rub shoulders with movers and shakers, attend presidential prayer breakfasts, speak at the National Press Club. Even the devil could see God was ill-advised, and in the wilderness suggested pulling rank, lording it over—playing the stuntman with a few spectacular miracles, dramatic rescue acts, dominion over the whole world.

No long-range vision. God declined, trotting past the great and leaping onto lesser mortals, flattening them with grace. Ignoring the Pope, dog licks the shabby nun who's there to wave from afar at the Holy Father.

Over and over, God plays the fool, sending the massed angel choir to a rabble of shepherds. Such an exotic, hard-to-book troupe—why send them to riffraff who would have been wowed by one shabby angel clutching a bit of tinsel? God over-the-top throws the party-to-end-all-parties for scum who had never been to so much as a kegger.

God, like dog, doesn't care whether they're wearing Brooks Brothers or bathrobes; doglike, God prefers 'em smelling a bit of sweat or pig, not Obsession or ceremonial soap. Neither dog nor God worry about proper accents, good grammar. God and dog celebrate. Or curl up and sympathize.

Buried like bones in a cosmic backyard, God has hidden these things from the wise and revealed them to infants. Searching high for God in mystical experiences, complicated revelations, asceticism, spiritual exercises? God is laid low, tucked under the mundane. Look down, not up—you can't see high enough—dig to find the treasure buried in your own backyard, called flesh.

*Three men, rich, from noble families, mid-fifties, wise—
seek exalted experience of God. Willing to travel.*

The wise men were looking high (not low) until their
necks were cricked. Dazzled by stars, they expected to be
bedazzled by God. Looking up, they played a game with
God: Hide the Holy One, and God is "it." Check Jerusalem?
The palace, of course. Where else could God be?

But there is a slip twixt cup and lip. God plays hard
to get, and as they quest, they are bent by their weakness, bowed to earth and flesh. Here they are bedazzled
by God's weakness—eyes blinded by God's dimness.
"Eureka!" they shout, befuddled. Look on flesh and
blood: It is Epiphany.

Epiphany means "looking upon the face," and the
church has made much of the wise men and Jesus
revealed to the nations. Instead, this: Epiphany is looking upon the face of God and reeling from its similarity
to our own.

The wedding at Cana is linked with epiphany because
Jesus is revealed—to sages here, to partying peasants
there. Here's God (enfleshed), sitting in Mary's lap; here's
God (enfleshed), eating lentils at a wedding. God in tangible form: King or villager (it doesn't matter) meet God,
welcome God, touch God, taste God.

Epiphany stands as the Feast Day of the
Disappointment—your chance to be underwhelmed.
Looking for God? Follow your nose to dirty diapers in

a cave. Want to see the long-awaited Messiah launch his ministry? Twirl your tongue around some *vin ordinaire* at a village wedding bash.

God the Party Animal

Cluny sat in the canoe, swam, and slept in the tent with me and my friend Jo in the Boundary Waters. First thing each morning, Cluny had to lick our faces. Cluny was distressed when, after all this closeness, Jo went back to England. They tried e-mail, but Cluny doesn't like it. She wants to smell her friend and taste her; Cluny prefers the tête-à-tête.

Face-to-face meetings, flesh touching flesh, banquets (with food that's eaten and wine that's drunk)—that's the revealed faith. You don't remember Passover, you eat it. You don't just hear the message of the angels, you tuck your robe up and belt off to see the baby. You don't ponder the Eucharist: God flung himself from the heights to be with us, so that we could eat God. That's how we plumb the depths of the tangible.

Try telling a dog that food is fleshly and insignificant, and she'll wag a tail at you patiently. Little wonder that during the Incarnation, the religious accused God of overeating and overdrinking—and with entirely the wrong people. In the Incarnation, God declares that stuff matters, that Platonism is wrong, spirituality inadequate.

God delights to feed us, to satisfy our hunger. Taught to starve ourselves, to count calories, to watch our cholesterol, to think salad—we assume God is abstemious. But God can't be stopped. Party, party, party.

One of Cluny's greatest joys is to lick me in the mouth. When she's leaning against me, if I laugh or speak, she'll make a lunge, touch my tongue with hers. People tell me she does that because her wolfish forebears regurgitated food to their young. Does Cluny think of me as her young who needs feeding?

Doglike, God says come and eat, come and drink, come and be satisfied. Banquets, feasts, parties: They are too good to refuse, so don't!

Why can't we be a little more spiritual, a little loftier, please God? What about Eastern mysticism or great ascetical philosophies that promote fasting to cleanse your system?

"I have come that you might have life and have it over the top," says God (John 10:10). Meagerness is not allowed. In the Incarnation, God fleshes out a net to gather things earthly and heavenly, the tangible and the spiritual.[4] Doglike, God fetches and parties. Order bread and, it's true, you are not given a stone. What comes to your table is triple layer chocolate cake—party fare.

That's the invitation: Come to the party. But consider carefully before you send your RSVP.

Helpful Hints for Possible Dog Lovers

(You Have Not Chosen Dog, Dog Has Chosen You)

In her housekeeping tips, Heloise offers wise counsel. Want a shiny house with minimum effort? Don't get a dog.

Dogs are a mess. A dog will rub your furniture to a shade of gray. Muddy paw prints on your kitchen floor will herald spring—no prizes for guessing who made them. You can't know when your dog will chew the carpet, but you can be sure she will. Unpredictability is your only guarantee with dog ownership. If you value tidiness and control, avoid getting a dog.

Dogs interfere. An acquaintance or stranger will arrive at your house, and your dog may greet her by licking her glasses.

We sat, one evening, chatting in the dining room, until a guest started groping under the table. Always the gracious hostess, I watched her for a few minutes, then asked, "Is something wrong?" "I took off my shoes under here," she said, "And now I can't find them." Cluny had taken them into the kitchen to give them a loving massage.

If you want to know where your shoes are, don't get a dog. Your dog will jump on beds, put her paw in your face to get your attention, chew your prized possessions. Your dog will roll in things.

Dog ownership leaves tracks all over your life. No more walking away from your house on some glorious vacation. A house sitter, a kennel—you need to think of your dog. When you pull out your suitcase, your dog will mope. When you're away, she might, like Cluny, poop and pee to let you know she's not happy—the wrath of dog.

Count the cost: No dog, and when you unlock your door, no one will rush you. Your beds will remain unwrinkled, pristine; no fluffs of dog hair will line your floors and peek out from beneath your radiators. No little clumps of dog poop will appear in your yard (or on your carpet). Excavation projects will not yawn open by the deck. Yes, if you want control, steer clear of dogs.

Let me reiterate: If you want control of your life, don't tangle with God. God is a mess, unpredictable, even dangerous. You will find God-tracks all over your life. You will be greeted in unexpected ways, knocked down at inopportune moments. You may find tables turned over. Nothing will be pristine and unwrinkled—you'll begin to wonder if anything belongs to you anymore. No! If you value tidiness, if you care for control, don't tangle with God.

People forget that a dog is not just a cuddly pup. The Royal Society for the Protection of Animals mounts billboards "A dog is for life—not just for Christmas" to remind us that a dog is not a toy. If you want a cuddly puppy, buy one that is stuffed. They are guaranteed not to poop, chew, or track muddy paws. Your lifestyle needn't change; your house will be tidy; you can leave that stuffed animal for years and it won't miss you.

How Much Is That Doggy in the Window?

Nicodemus came to Jesus: "I'm thinking about getting a puppy—what do you think?"

"You—a teacher of Israel—you don't know?" Jesus said.

Nicodemus shook his head and Jesus said, "Be aware that you are not deciding about whether or not to get a puppy. You're embarking on a whole new venture that will change you forever. You are entwining your life with dog. The wind whooshes around and you don't know where it's headed and you can't tell it where to go. In the same way, when you get a dog, your control is over. Are you sure, being a teacher (and, you must admit, a bit of an anal retentive control freak), you want to make this kind of commitment?"[5]

The rich young man came to Jesus, eager for real life, and Jesus told him he needed to give up control. Get a dog and let it chew through your stuff. Poor guy—he walked away sorrowing. He knew he wasn't a dog kind of guy.

Dogs will shake all over you. They throw themselves in the water and scatter their blessings everywhere.

Dog Chooses You

So you're convinced that it's not just puppy love. You claim you're ready for surprises.

You can never be fully prepared, God only knows, for the changes dog will bring to your life.

You don't have to know a lot about dog ownership to get a dog. Your knowledge of dog anatomy can be limited, your understanding of dog psychology abysmal. Often we've been given the impression that we can get ourselves ready for life with dog, by getting our acts together (engaging in excellent behavior, making an elegant profession). Sometimes our preparations become our protection against the grace of God.

I think, maybe, yes, I'd like to see Cluny and maybe even ask her if she'd go for a walk with me. Of course, I have to get up the nerve to even approach her—I've heard dog has very high standards and won't go with just anyone. She might disapprove of me, think I'm inadequate. Maybe I should wait and ask her later . . . that's what I'll do, I'll spend some time getting ready.

Perhaps new walking shoes would help, a new jogging outfit. That's it. I invest in new tennies, a matching jacket.

But, I think, if she doesn't want to go with me, with my new clothes, maybe I could never in a million years be good enough. I imagine myself approaching Cluny and picture her response.

Cluny hears that I'm considering talking to her. She rolls her eyes and asks her secretary to take a letter:

Madam:

It has come to my attention that you have made frivolous, even sarcastic, comments lately and have been guilty of letting the car run almost out of gas so that your partner has to fill it. You have also addressed me without proper reverence. I'm not even going to mention that second piece of chocolate turtle cake when you weren't even hungry for one. You know that you cannot approach me until you set these matters straight. Make sure that you have taken care of them entirely before I hear your footsteps on the sidewalk, your knock on the front door.

> Always your loving dog,
> Cluny

Perhaps a fitness plan to ensure a new spring in my step? I know—I need to know more about walking or perhaps about dogs. I could check the library: a course—the community college offers courses on dogs. . . .

Exhausted, in a moment of forgetfulness, I pick up the leash. Cluny scrambles to her feet, dancing the whole body wag. She leaps, she runs to the door. She is ready to go anywhere with me. How could I have forgotten that?

Doglike, God has no black book. God-like, dog takes the slightest indication on my part and multiplies it. The spark: the prayer, "God help me," a response to an altar call, a word that even sounds like "w-a-l-k"—and before we know it, we're in a blaze of joyful, tail-wagging pleasure.

I may say it over and over: no. Get down. No dogs allowed. I'm sorry we don't take pets. Stay. Down. I hesitate just once, and there is God, at my elbow, ready to greet me. The crinkle of a plastic bag, the tread of tennis shoes, the word w-a-l-k, and Cluny is up, leaning over the gate, wagging in her willingness.

Dog Bless Us Every One!

(Where Love Is, There Is Dog)

God's breath, Chinook-like, thaws us. God bounces on the bed with a wake-up kiss. Ours is to allow the greeting, not to shrink from the loving paws. But what can you expect when you meet Dog? Well, for one thing, dog will not want to let you go.

The Dogged Love of Dog

Lyn owned a border collie named Jocko who welcomed people to the house with open paws. Jocko, however, harbored a deep instinctual urge to bite anyone who tried to leave. Lyn had to put the dog in the kitchen when guests moved toward the front door so that Jocko wouldn't nip their heels in a last-ditch effort to keep them from leaving. And it's true: God gets teeth into you and it's hard to get away.

When I greet a family member or visitor with a hug, within nanoseconds, one of us feels large paws on our back. If we stand before a meal to hold hands and pray, Cluny worms herself into the center of the group. When two or three are gathered, dog is in their midst.

Dog wants us all to be together. Cluny walks around the cabin, sniffing . . . and she's pleased. 97, 98, 99, 100 . . . yes, all present and accounted for. Then she can flop down, happy. The great banquet at the end of time will be a party because all the beloved will be present and accounted for.

Cluny hates September because people go away to college. One day, it seems, she has her whole family there; then one packs up and goes, and now another.

As a retriever, Cluny wants to bring stuff back. If someone throws a rock into a lake, she swims around, plunging her head under the water trying to find that damn thing. When visitors leave, she looks for them for a few days, then settles down to wait and dog-dream her Christmas welcomes.

Like Cluny, we dream of meetings. We dream of heaven as a place to meet loved ones, great saints. The disciples on the road to Emmaus met a stranger and bared their souls to him. As he tore open a loaf of bread, "their eyes were opened and they recognized him" (Luke 24:31). As creatures of flesh and blood, we want our meetings to be sacramental—we want to hug our friends, to make love with our love. Cluny dreams of planting her paws on Andrew's shoulders, nibbling his neck; she dreams of knocking Stephen onto the floor to lick his face.

What is hell but separation? Separation from God, yes, but from others too, as C.S. Lewis portrayed a vast hell where people move further and further apart because they cannot bear to be together.[6] Hell becomes an eternity of not-meeting. Perhaps this is why child kidnapping strikes us as the ultimate horror: the hours, days, weeks, months, and years of never knowing, of not-meeting. Motherdog will fight to protect her pup, will draw blood to get to her young.

Cluny is a jealous dog; she firmly believes that we should have no other dogs before her. If I greet a neighbor's dog on the sidewalk, she wiggles between and looks at me—why do you need anyone else? If the cat jumps onto my lap, she watches carefully. I am my beloved's and she is mine, thinks the jealous dog.

God jealously longs for meeting, offers us welcome in exchange for the hell of separation. We can trust the retriever dog, because she always remembers the ones she loves.

Marked as Dog's Own Forever

Dog never forgets her own. Even years later, dog catches the slightest whiff of an old friend and she knows . . . she knows. Just as some dogs mark trees to show their ownership, Cluny must have marked us as her own forever.

Sometimes at a baptism people tell their stories, testify to how bad they'd become before they turned to God. They've got it upside down. Baptism is better understood as God's mark on us, the stain of God's grace. Years later, sniffing along, God can smell those who carry the sign: We are marked as Christ's own forever.

No, it's not your story about how you found God, or my story about coming to God: It's always a dog story, about the bounce and breath of God. In the hands of God, two fish make a feast; pale water makes vintage wine. That's what God is like.

Saul, the prodigal son, Levi, Zacchaeus—God sees the spark and is there, blowing, blowing. Take a little, such a little, and sprinkle with God. You end up with baskets of leftovers.

Learning to Live with Dog

No one would call Cluny standoffish. The adjectives "cool," "reserved," or "snobby" do not spring to mind. No wonder dogs are brought in to reach out to Alzheimer's patients or the dreadfully traumatized—it's hard to resist the nuzzle and lick of love. Cluny has never thought, "Okay, enough people for today . . . just leave me alone." As Cluny is her dogself, free to be entirely doggish, she's an inspiration to me. I crawl up to her on the kitchen floor and put my head on her side and feel her breathing.

Cluny assumes the best in people. She knows that if someone heads for the door, it is likely because they want to take her for a nice long w-a-l-k. If she hears a bread bag crumple, it probably means they have it in mind to give her a little something to snack on. She knows she's loveable, and so of course folks will want to go out with her or give her little treats.

But if no one heads for the door or picks up the leash, Cluny finds ways to remind her family that it's about time for fellowship in the open air. She subtly brings her leash and puts it on your feet. Or she might stare and stare and stare and stare and stare until you say, "Okay, darn it. We'll go, but just for a short one. . . ." And then you get outside . . . and the moon is picking up little sparkles on the snow or the lake is a dusky purple or the wind is tossing the branches of an old tree and you notice for the first time that the swirls of its trunk look like a van Gogh sky. As you walk on, you realize that you wouldn't be out here without dog. No dog, and you might have forgotten what was most important—fresh air, stars, time with dog.

But even as you enjoy the winter evening, you know that dog is present in it more than you can ever be. You don't know who came by earlier today, but dog does: She picks up a scent and follows it. She stops and sniffs for a minute, and you know that if she wanted to, she could tell you a whole story about that piece of earth and who's passed there and why. We both come in from a walk with fresh air glancing off us like blessings, but she has a story to tell. Walking with dog is an Emmaus experience: Each time our eyes are opened and we see something afresh.

You come in and put the leash and the coat away. Now what? Dog just wants to sit with you. Often, Cluny finds that she's accidentally slipped right up onto the couch, which means she can put her head in your lap. When you stir, she licks you. You could stay like that forever, as far as Cluny is concerned—you and the dog who loves you—sitting and snoring and dog-dreaming dreams of homecoming and rescue.

10

Rescue Dog and Her Startling Rescue Attempts

(Running from the Hound of Heaven)

Dogs will search for people buried in earthquake rubble for eighteen or twenty hours a day, without slowing down. "What makes them keep looking when they must be tired and hungry?" I heard an interviewer ask a man who owns a team of rescue dogs. "That's just the way dogs are," he answered. "They assume that any person they find will be a new friend, so they can hardly wait to sniff them out."

Rescue dog scratches anxiously at the door of the abandoned barn, paws at the beam that has fallen across the old mine shaft. She whines, desperate to get to her beloved.

If I sneeze, Cluny leaps up. A distress signal, she thinks, throwing herself into my rescue. I'm experienced;

I know what's coming. Sneeze and brace yourself for flying dog. But the unsuspecting might be bowled over by her sudden rescue attempt.

We call her Rescue Dog. Coursing through her veins is the blood of dogs who have rescued children from burning houses, pulled women from turbulent rivers, hauled men from quicksand. Perhaps her great, great grandsire discovered a young woman caught by an avalanche just in time to administer a swig of brandy from a neck cask.

Just as well: I need all the rescuing I can get. Late September in the Boundary Waters is moose-mating time, and a bull moose stomped and snorted around our tent two nights running. Cluny's growl (she assumed) kept us safe from a ton of horny moose meat.

Many dogs take their role as protectors very seriously, barking at any sign of danger, such as a mail flap clinking or a newspaper hitting the door. Cluny barks once a month, and when she does, she looks around surprised—who said that? We say she's a member of the "bark of the month club," but even so, Cluny's bark is worse than her bite.

What doggish qualities make them rescuers? Cluny has a great set of ears. She hears the cries of the lost, the quick intake of breath before the sneeze. Her sense of smell is terrific. And she's faithful. She doesn't get bored and move on. Hearing her owner's cries, she's not about to curl up and go to sleep.

Collapsed mine shafts and avalanches are not much compared to the barriers we erect against the seeking God. We bury ourselves in quicksand or snow; we wind up comatose. Rescue dog must perform some startling feats. But that's okay: Anything to get us to the party.

Startling Rescue Attempt #1:
Rescue Dog Saves Someone
Dressed in His/Her Sunday Best

We hide from rescue dog in an amazing array of protective garments, so fully garbed we can hardly waddle toward God. Buckled and zipped into our Sunday best, even rescue dog struggles to liberate us.

Rescue dog chewed off the Velcro closings and laces on Saul's clothes as he walked along the Damascus road (Acts 9:1–9). But first she had to knock him flat. There was Saul, strolling along, swaddled in self-righteousness, mouth set in a grim line. His duty was not pleasant, but someone has to be responsible for stamping out heresy— and, after all, life is no party. All this trash about Messiah welcoming tax collectors, sinners, women, riffraff!

God has standards, after all . . . and, suddenly, paws knock the wind out of him. He feels his clothes gently pulled off and finds himself dazed by warm breath, soothed by a thorough tongue.

Damascus road dust in his mouth, Saul lies low, flattened by love. Years later, Paul wrote about "the love of God poured into our hearts" (Romans 5:5). Prone and helpless, the spit of God floods away years of good habits, excellent law-keeping, so that Paul can remind believers all over Asia Minor that they are no longer outsiders. They've been brought close, God using flesh to knock down walls. They've been licked by extravagant, impractical love.

Saul knows he should get up; his comrades will think he's lost his mind. But somehow he doesn't care about standing on his own two feet—he's done it for so long. No, he would just as soon be carried. He feels himself picked up by a soft mouth.

Like Saul, we don our good behavior, compulsive activity, a firm sense of our own responsibility. After all, if I don't do it, who will? With help from pastors and parents, we've fashioned ourselves into little Pharisees, dressed in our "Sunday best." This is God's house— whisper if you speak at all—quietly, shhhhhh! We've learned our lessons well: God prefers me if my hair's combed, my suit pressed, my dress ironed (shoes polished, little bag matching). If you want God's love, you must behave. God runs a tight ship—doesn't want to be associated with someone like you—you are not careful enough about your language, not always kind to others. If and when you improve your manners, then maybe, maybe a meeting could be set up. . . .

Why do we think we need our Sunday best to meet God? Cluny doesn't understand dressing for success. With dogs, what you see is what you get. Cluny's wardrobe contains no power suits, no sexy outfits. She never primps in front of a mirror. It's possible that she may not know her color season! Cluny thumps her tail to remind me that she loves me. Makeup on? Matching socks? Cluny doesn't care.

God, like dog, doesn't dress up. Drag your child to church in her Sunday best. Church turns out to be the hangout of a God bedraggled who hasn't managed to pull on any clothes this morning.

Startling Rescue Attempt #2:
Rescue Dog Saves Someone Floundering in Honor

The story is told about two dogs meeting on the street. Jack, a streetwise mongrel, introduces himself. He asks Charlotte, a perfectly groomed poodle, about herself.

"I won Best in Show for the last two years at the regionals. My owner has the silver platters above the fireplace, and I got so many championship points that we're heading to the Westminster Kennel Club show in New York next week. You may not know that the Westminster is by invitation only, the second oldest sporting event in the country after the Kentucky Derby, and I may make Best of Breed. My master wants Best of Group there, though he knows I'll never make Best of Show. . . . This ear is almost an eighth of an inch longer than the other. . . ."

Jack looks at her and shakes his head: "It's all crap, Charlotte, all crap."

Jack's right. It's hard to imagine a dog caring more about a silver cup than a walk, more about a ribbon than a scratch behind the ears.

Our ribbons, our silver platters, our honor: They are all crap. They are the emperor's new clothes, the Wizard of Oz's tricks behind a curtain. Rescue dog approaches. She sniffs, and, yes, there is someone under all that manure.

General, professor, bishop—honor is the false glue that holds everyone in place so we know who is worthy. Chair, Best Actress, Nobel Prize winner—all are incandescent paisley catching the light, swirling, swirling. Surgeon, president, reverend—we cannot tear our eyes away. The slightest breeze, and poof, they are gone.

Rescue dog wants to pull her beloved out of the excrement, to rip the medals off and trample on the academic garb. Throw that fancy suit away, dispatch your surgeon's outfit, put your bishop's regalia in the children's costume box.

Honor and respectability demand we look up to them; glory peeks out beneath our feet, where God has squirreled it. Gawking at celebrities, we miss glimpses of glory. Trying to scale the ladder—of academia, the corporation, the military, the church—we look upward and onward. The apostle Paul said he counted all his accomplishments as dung, compared to knowing God (Philippians 3:7–9). Glory, remember, is tucked in the ordinary, where human flesh dwells.

Rescue dog can't force people to be rescued. God leaps the barriers, parts the seas, scratches at the door. Medieval theologians discussed whether God could make a stone too heavy for himself to lift. Often the church has made stones and bound them to people, stones that try even the strength of God. We cling—rigor-mortis–like—to these stones, holding on, we think, for dear life, sinking while rescue dog swims nearby, mournfully watching the bubbles, until she pulls us out.

Your Dog Is Too Small

(Let Go and Let Dog)

Dog gives no thought for the morrow. She is here now, and now is everything. You can take a dog for a walk, and if she hears her leash rattle an hour later, she's set to go, jumping with excitement. "You've already had one," I say, and she looks at me puzzled. Well, maybe—she remembers having one once, but that was a long time ago, probably last week; it doesn't matter really. The fact is that was then and now is now, and now is perfect for a walk. Cluny knows what we forget: Life is here and now, the only place where we touch eternity. Listen—the birds are singing and it smells good, so let's go. Now is party time!

My daughter and I drive back, from even the grocery store. "Well, do you suppose Cluny will greet us warmly when we come home?" "Nah, probably she'll be bored, raise one eyebrow. Ho hum, you again." We brace ourselves when we open the door. We know what dog is like—short on proportion, prudence, strategy. Tumbling, body surfing, Cluny leaps up. Just like her, God is a mess.

Institutions try to be practical, responsible. In Acts 1, the guys gather for an important subcommittee meeting. "Let's see, Jesus said to wait, so what shall we do? He couldn't have meant just wait. I guess we're short one of the twelve; so let's elect a new one, how 'bout, and that'll get things ready to go." God confounds them, chuckling as Spirit bowls them over. Gale-force wind, a fire raging out of control, a torrential downpour of languages: Luke's best efforts to describe Pentecost. The tiny match catches, and soon it is a wall of flame, crackling sparks fly off the top, billows of smoke. Of course you can't pour a cup of water on it or throw a blanket over it. Run for your life! Onlookers can only conclude the disciples are drunk—they're so noisy and high-spirited.

No wonder Trinity Sunday follows hot on the heels of Pentecost in the liturgical calendar: one way to put out fires of the Spirit. Compared to the Spirit, the Trinity is tame. "Damn," says the church, "those rivers of living water."

Human desire to domesticate dog shows itself in the painfully overdressed dog, the dog whose embarrassment is not hidden by the smart cloak, the plaid hair ribbon, the stylish cut. This is dog made in our image, after our likeness. Yet we cannot hide dog's fundamental doggish-ness. Dogs feel the wildness of their forebears. They spot the moon and wonder if they should howl. "Speak," we say, wanting to hear dog speak on our command.

The church has tried desperately to domesticate the Spirit. "Sit." "You can't do it that way. No, you have to be converted first and then receive the Spirit." "Stay." "The Spirit's role is to convict you of sin." "Roll over." "The Spirit was necessary before the canon of Scripture was complete." "Heel."

God delighted, God reckless, God debauched—the generous luxury of God, incongruous with much reli-gious experience. The Spirit is unpredictable—living water overflowing banks, waterfalls washing, flooding. Alpine meadows teeming with flowers, bees, butter-flies, grace upon grace. Drenched in spirit, flowing over, around and through you, making you dance as you never thought you could. You shout, you run, you hug, you tango. Someone lets dog in (or out) and she joins, leap-ing, licking, wagging, romping, frolicking.

The Spirit is embarrassing. Pentecost is like a Down Syndrome child, speaking in full voice during a concert, "I'm having such a good time. I'm very happy." Pentecost is the one-year-old flapping arms and legs when Dad walks in. Someone needs to teach these folks moderation.

Help 'em to not show so much emotion; teach 'em some manners, for heaven's sake.

Company in the living room, nibbling on appetizers, chatting politely, but someone has left the kitchen door open, and Cluny makes a break for it. She leaps up on the man wearing his best work suit. She sprawls across the lap of the woman who doesn't like dogs. There's no question about it—dog is here.

Respectable older siblings struggle to let go and let dog. The wild Spirit tugs at their Sunday best, grasps at their medals, tears at their Calvin Klein suits. These first-born clutch their clothing, fearful. Please, please, don't make me go to your party.

Martha can't give up her outstanding cuisine (Luke 10:38–42), her award-winning table settings; the older brother to the prodigal hates to let go of all his accumulated responsibility points (Luke 15:11–32); Simon the Pharisee can't drop his respectability and control (Luke 7:36–50).

"Excuse me, please," says Martha, "isn't my entertaining important?" "But what about all my years of being good?" wails the older brother. "I want to get this straight, to understand the rules," says one of the twelve. "If my brother or sister sins against me, tell me exactly, Lord, how many times must I forgive?" "Who, precisely, is first in the kingdom of God? Who," discuss the twelve, "will sit at your right hand and at your left? Will I be able to tell by their outfits? What commandments do I need to keep? How can I be expected to perform right if no one will tell me what I need to do?" (Matt 18:21–22; Luke 22:28–30).

Walking from the train, he knew what the evening held: some web-surfing, particularly new investment sites—pretty daring stuff, these commodities—then check the wine cellar, perhaps forty-five minutes on the exercise bike and then bed.

He turns the corner and freezes. The house is lit up, and he can hear the stereo from the street. Squatters! Some crazy kids, it sounds like. Oh, God, no! His brother?

Standing on the porch, his dad smiles and lifts his hand. The light glints from that greeting like a nuclear flash. He looks down and sees his hand as if in an X-ray, white bones on a gray background. His new gray suit sweeps back with the wind, and he crumples to the ground. His dad picks him up, holding him, rocking and speaking soft words, "Let me help you inside. You'll feel better in a few minutes. Your brother's home. . . ."

"Let me go. . . . Let me go. . . . I'm needed back at the office. . . ." He struggles from his father's arms, running toward the station. On the train, he sits with his arms folded across his chest, his eyes closed, trembling.

They'll be missed, I guess, those older siblings. It's hard not to feel for them. They thought they knew the rules, and goodness knows they'd been taught them, and then the reckoning system changed.

The church dreads Pentecost, miracles, apparitions. Church authorities hope against hope that no one will see an appearance of Mary. What a nuisance, all these uneducated peasants, expecting to encounter the divine. They won't take *no* for an answer.

Neither will the divine. Over and over God does the unexpected, making himself unpopular with the church offices who have spiritual life in neat files until God comes along. Enthusiasm, Bishop Butler suggested to John Wesley, is a terrible thing, a very terrible thing.

"I beg to differ," says God. Enthusiasm, dog knows, is at the heart of love, carrying you away so that you can't help but wag. Pentecost is a dance of greeting: the whole body wag, a wiggle of warmth. "Hi, hi, hi. Do you want to come along? I'm down," says Jesus, "and the Spirit is out." Down, Jesus sports with sinners. Out, Spirit polkas with folks who've said *yes* to the party.

Without the overwhelming presence of the Spirit, God might have stayed bound, never shaking off the womb's tight comfort. Dog concentrates, her back smooth with water flowing over, her lungs tearing air. Then, feet on ground, breaking out of the water, she shakes, laughing—don't mind if I do shake on you, share my joy, my stick, my life! *Spirito Generoso*—and out God tumbles, somersaults, handsprings, making everything touched turn to more. A few fish and a loaf or two? Pass them out. Verily, you have heard it said unto you, "Watch out, there's barely enough to go around." But I say to you, "Share and have fun, and there will be plenty. In fact, what will we do with the leftovers?"

Spirito Generoso blows, and you can't stop it, twisting your hair and pressing your eyelashes. You spin and leap, as if you had the body of Baryshnikov—all the dancer's joy and abandon without the excruciating years *en pointe*, the months not eating croissants. You can dance because Spirit lofts your limbs and makes you wild. You fly, body flung as wide as possible—catching Spirit wind in deep gulps.

12

If You Can't Make It to the Party, Dog Comes to You

(Nearer My Dog to Thee)

Rescue dog has failures. In a doggish sitcom, hero-dog always emerges victorious. We've never heard the music fade with the words: "And his beloved expired in the old mine shaft," with a close-up of rescue dog shaking his head mournfully. But off the big screen, rescue dog is often a bust as a rescuer.

Cluny is a wonderful animal, but she can't knot ropes, and her paws make it difficult for her to dial 911. Mouth-to-mouth resuscitation is not her strength (dog-food breath or not), and she'd be a disaster at the Heimlich Maneuver, since her leaping is better than her embrace. She can't drive an ambulance or don a smoke mask. I try to picture Cluny training for an emergency ambulance job, paws fumbling, mouth pursed in concentration.

Truth is, I'm not sure I finally expect rescue. I seldom find myself in a collapsed mineshaft. If I did, rescue would be nice, but mostly I'd want to know I wasn't alone. Usually I don't need someone's dexterous paws to untie the ropes or someone's breath breathing into me: What I need is a wagging tail and some warm dog breath against my ear. Cluny doesn't give superficial advice, ask too many questions, or try to distract me with small talk. God-like, doglike, she's there.

The most pressing challenge to faith never changes: Why does God allow awful things to happen? Where is God when it hurts?

Where Is Dog When It Hurts?

When I call Cluny, she streaks toward me. I brace myself, remembering a woman on crutches who confided that her legs were broken by her dog's boisterous greeting.

When we swim, Cluny sits on the shore, quivering with excitement until Susannah whoops. Then Cluny bolts toward the water, dives in, and paddles, head up, paws moving like pistons, tail lashing from side to side. When she gets to Susannah, she licks her face and then goes to work affecting a rescue.

If Cluny and Stephen are sitting on a dock and Stephen dives in, Cluny sails in after him. Once she landed on Stephen's head. Ninety pounds of dog holding him under, she started her rescue effort, yanking his hair with her teeth. Stephen, I'm pleased to report, survived the best efforts of rescue dog.

We emerge from swimming with Cluny bearing the stigmata, the marks of her love—scratches on our backs, necks, arms where she paddled toward us to greet or rescue, unaware of her own strength. In God's dramatic rush to receive us, perhaps God scratches, oblivious to God's powerful paws. Could it be that in God's enthusiasm, God forgets our thin-skinnedness and bumps us over like bowling pins? Or is it that the underdog vision gives God a different view of broken legs? The good book says that God remembers that we are but grass (Ps 103:13–16), but perhaps God (absentmindedly distracted by love) occasionally forgets.

Rescue Dog Is There

People survive terrible tragedies, and there's no knowing why these things happen. But in the midst of awful circumstances, people often testify to a sense of presence. Fully present, doglike, God is there, seldom speaking unless it is an incantation deeper than words.

Heather's father was in his early fifties when his cancer was diagnosed. It spread quickly, and like many people near death, he seemed to retreat into himself. The family sat with him, but he paid little attention to them.

One day, he was near the end. There in the hospital room, they had all wept so much there were no tears left to cry. Suddenly, his face cleared and his eyes opened; he sat up, and on his face was a look of inexpressible joy. "Look," he cried, "look!" He laughed and died.

Cluny can carry a wounded animal without hurting it. Yes, it's in her mouth, but it's Cluny who's carrying, and she's endlessly gentle. God carries with a gentle mouth, doglike, and people testify to a sense of being softly carried by the nurturing mouth of God, soaked in the loving spit of God.

This potent amulet against the powers of darkness (within and without) is all we have against the worst that life has to offer. The charm doesn't protect us as we'd hoped; yes, your father will sicken; yes, you could be hurt in a car accident. But there is Presence, a wet nose in your hand, a tail thumping on the floor next to the bed. The beloved is there, and that is the deepest of the deep magic. It is this incantation that we must write on our hearts, pressing hard so that it marks over the lie—that only the beautiful find love—that we learned so well. Dog is in the midst of us and we shall not be moved.

Cluny licks my tears and nibbles my neck when I weep. She grunts when I rub her ears, chanting for me a plainsong of her love. She charms my fears and bids my sorrows cease. I listen to her because she whispers the secret about God—that God is loving and I am loved. What more do I need to know?

Dog jumps fully into joy and sorrow. She does not know how to hold herself back, just in case. She doesn't look around wondering who's watching, check her fur and makeup in case her one-ing with someone is being caught on film.

Life is full of great joys and terrible sorrows. Often our approach is analgesic—drug the pain, avoid it, run from it, forget it. Not dog. Jesus refuses the proffered vinegar, so deeply is he immersed in our pain. Dog of sorrows, what a name. . . .

Doglike, God doesn't get wedged in the artificially sweetened, Disney layer of life. In the ICU, the mortuary, the nursing home—there is God, muzzle against cheek. In the joy of friend meeting friend, courageous choices, tender moments—there is God.

Rescue Dog Gives Up on Extraordinary Measures (Nothing Can Separate Us from the Love of Dog)

As a rescue dog, Cluny is a bust. You see, she's not big on extraordinary measures. Sure, she'll sit with you (or on you). If you jump into the sea (thinking you are going for a swim), she'll jump on top of you so you do need rescuing. Heaven knows, she'd love to carry you, but you're too big.

No, Cluny is not a great rescuer. Better rescuers race in, equipment in hand, all efficiency—where's the problem? They set up machines, take measurements, and rush, sirens wailing, through the streets. They wheel patients into the hospital importantly, put them on multiple monitors with numbers and dials they can watch. They maintain the patient's vital signs, help them hang on for dear life—if "life" is a permanent vegetative state. If time is a lockstep through eternity, then we must check off as many heartbeats, as many breaths as we can.

Having hoed so many fields and been so responsible, the prodigal's older brother was in a prime vegetative state. Dog runs into the field and invites him to the party. He doesn't care for dogs, their enthusiasm, their lack of attention to detail. The church likes to hook its patients up to monitors, where its staff can graph venial and mortal sins, numbers of souls led to Jesus, hours spent in Bible study, until the patients are only half there, in a permanent vegetative state.

Rescue dog doesn't do extreme measures. The most extreme measures have already been done—tumbling, stripping, rolling. It's enough for rescue dog to be down and out. It's enough to be there, dog with us.

Rescuers rush in and hitch up machines. Dog rushes in and licks your face. Presumably, God could pull out machines, machines beyond our wildest expectations—truly *deus ex machina*—to deliver us. God could do that, but it seems that often God, doglike, prefers simply being there to extraordinary measures.

Deus ex machina—the unexpected, unrealistic, almost laughable deliverance—has the bad name it does in literary circles because that's not the way we know the world to be. *Deus ex canina* comes in and sits, tail thumping occasionally, muzzle on neck, occasional lick on hand until the heart stops.

It's all over: The graph lines on the machines fall flat. The rescuers shake their heads and start unhooking.

Deep within, far beyond their most sensitive monitors, the stilled heart quivers. That sound? What is it?

A scratch from the other side of glory's door, a whimper of welcome. The yelp of greeting warns you. Brace yourself: This is the moment you've been waiting for. Prepare to meet thy dog.

Notes

1. Anselm, from Cur Deus homo, I xi–xx, in *S. Anselmi Opera Omnia*, ed. F.S. Schmitt, vol.2 (Edinburgh: Nelson, 1946), 68.3–89.32, 99.3–132.6 3.

2. Dorothy Sayers, *The Mind of the Maker* (New York: HarperSanFrancisco, 1987), 25. Originally published in 1941 by Harcourt, Brace.

3. William Armstrong, *Sounder* (New York: HarperCollins, 1970), 108.

4. Adapted from blessing from *Service of Nine Lessons and Carols*.

5. John 3:1–15, author paraphrase.

6. C. S. Lewis, *The Great Divorce* (New York: HarperCollins, 1946).